LETTERS FROM GOD

Monica Gilk

ISBN 979-8-88685-530-2 (paperback)
ISBN 979-8-88685-531-9 (digital)

Christian Faith Publishing
832 Park Avenue
Meadville, PA 16335
www.christianfaithpublishing.com

Printed in the United States of America

I hope everyone who reads this book I wrote receives from it. How this book came about was over three years ago. I was very young, probably around the age of eighteen. I remember it like yesterday. I was in my room watching *Finding Nemo*, the Walt Disney movie, and things about God and this movie were like relating together, to myself, then I had this urge to write. I didn't know what about until the end. It's funny how God uses anyone. If you know me, I personally can't spell or read good. But if God wants you to do something he wants done, he will equip you just like he did with me just now. It took me a very long time to finish this book.

After the *Finding Nemo* story, I couldn't stop writing whenever I got the urge. The enemy got into my head many times, made me feel stupid and like, I'm only a young girl, no one was going to read this if I turned all my notes into a book. I got attacked many times because the Lord told me maybe a year or two after to write a book about what he had been telling me to write. So after all the years of writing and believing the enemy's lies, I finally started blocking out his lies and listened to the King's voice. So this whole book was him telling me what to write about, just to spread his Gospel.

So I truly hope you receive from this book and get to know Jesus, our Lord and Savior. And if you don't know him, and you want to, all you have got to do is say the sinner's prayer which is, "Dear Lord Jesus, I know I am a sinner. I believe you died for my sins.

Right now, I turn from my sins and open the door of my heart and life. I confess you as my personal Lord and Savior. Amen."

Introduction

This book is a very eye-opening, awakening your spirit book. How this all started was, one day, a girl was lying down in her room, and she had the urge to write. She didn't know what she was going to write, but all she knew was that it was something for the Lord. And by the time she would be done writing, she would sit back and look, and it would be a whole page. She didn't know what to call it at first. Notes, reminder, maybe even letters from God. Ever since that one night she was lying in her bed, she couldn't stop writing. Every time she got the urge to write, she would have to write whatever the Lord would tell her to write. So I hope you receive and enjoy what I call *Letters from God*. In this book, you will find encouraging messages, restoring your faith and knowing who the true enemy is.

Jesus Is Always Looking Out

I'm lying down, watching *Finding Nemo*. And as I'm watching *Finding Nemo,* I realized in the part of the movie when Marlin was going to take Nemo to school, he went out of his house three or four times, checking to see if it's safe to leave and go to school and thought he was nuts for checking a hundred times before they left. As I'm watching *Finding Nemo*, something came to me and said, "That's like Jesus watching us and checking our surroundings for our own safety."

And we don't know why, just as Nemo didn't know, just as we don't know why Jesus does what he does, but it's for our own good. Another part of the movie, something came to me where Nemo goes to a drop-off, and when Marlin heard Nemo going to the drop-off, he panicked and went swimming as fast as he could to stop Nemo from going to the drop-off. Everyone knew the drop-off was a bad place in the movie, so in my mind, I thought we were Nemo, and Marlin was Jesus, always looking out for his child, looking for the best, and not wanting harm to come to his child either.

So my point is when Marlin heard Nemo was going to the drop-off, and he went swimming to him, I took it as Jesus came swimming to us to save us and tried and stopped us from going on the wrong path. And one more thing came to me. So after Nemo left and didn't listen to his father, he got taken, and Marlin never gave up through the whole movie to find his son and bring him home. This is like Jesus who is never going to give up on us when we leave him and turn our backs on him and don't listen, just like how Nemo didn't listen to Marlin and still went out and touched the boat off the drop-off.

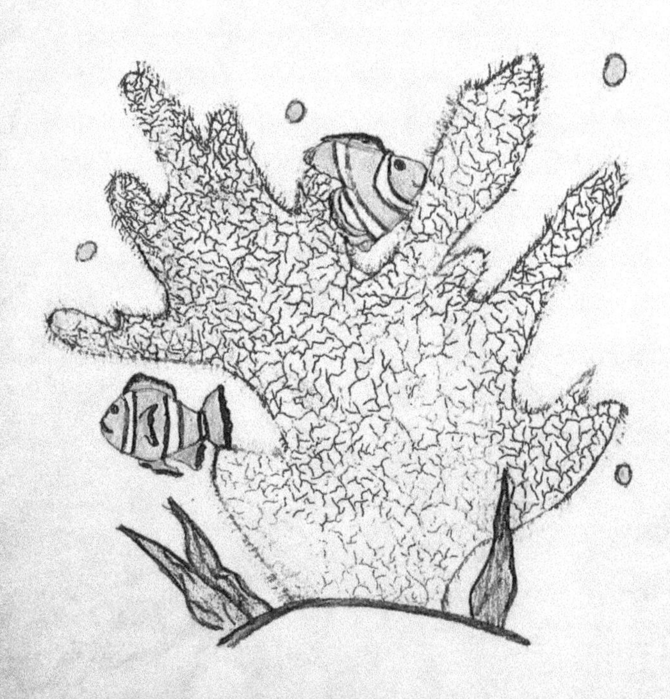

Verses 10-14 See that you do not despise one of these little ones. For I tell you that their angels in heaven always see the face of my Father in heaven. What do you think? If a man owns a hundred sheep, and one of them wanders away, will he not leave the ninety-nine on the hills and go to look for the one that wandered off? And if he finds it truly, I tell you he is happier about that one sheep than about the ninety-nine that did not wander off. In the same way your Father in heaven is not willing that any of these little ones should perish. (Matthew 18:10-14 NIV)

Verse 15 I am with you and will watch over you wherever you go, and I will bring you back to this land. I will not leave you until I have done what I have promised you. (Genesis 28:15 NIV)

Verse 8 I will instruct you and teach you in the way you should go I will counsel you with my loving eye on you. (Psalms 32:8 NIV)

Know Your Enemy

I was just thinking this morning, we are never ever going to get away from Satan tempting us, distracting, and getting on our nerves. You'll never run from it. You can't. That's what he does and that's what he's supposed to do, to get under our skin to make us get aggravated and overthink so we can never grow. The more you grow, the more he comes after you. So never stop growing. God will give you strength to keep on going. The devil is a very tricky slick guy. He comes in, and you don't even know it until you realize what just happened or you realize that was temptation if you didn't give in. Sometimes, he uses people, your own family, to get on your nerves or make you think bad thoughts about your family members so you can never forgive them and have love in your heart for them. You'll just have hate and bitterness in your heart, and that is what he wants. Everything bad he wants and nothing of God.

He is the exact opposite of the Lord Jesus, who is the light, and he is the dark. Jesus wants to give you the world. The devil wants to give you nothing but torture. Jesus is love, happiness, peace, everything good, and wants us to be just like him and love one another so we can be just like him. But now the devil wants everything the opposite. He wants us to be not happy, not having love in our hearts. He wants us to live in fear and doubt. This guy has nothing good to offer us, but yet, we still fall into his trap because we are sinners and don't realize until we fall for his trick.

It could be a small trick or a big trick. It doesn't matter. We should be smarter to know better. But we're humans, and we fall for it because we don't think about it. We don't give it enough time to get convicted or have a second thought about this. But if we do get enough time, we still don't listen because it sounds good to us, and we will just say at the end, "Oh Lord, forgive me."

He will forgive me. He loves me. Yeah, he loves you and always will forgive you, but you have to fear the Lord. You can't take it for granted. He didn't have to send his Son to die on the cross for you, and Jesus didn't have to die for you either. He could have said, "No, I'm not going to earth to die for people who are just going to keep doing wrong."

But that's where his love, kindness, and grace came in. He loves us so he sent his Son to die for us on this earth, and Jesus loves us so much he actually came and got hung on a cross with nails for us, just so we wouldn't go to hell and burn and suffer forever, but so we can live with him forever in his kingdom. The Lord has so much for us to offer, but we don't listen and fall for Satan's tricks again. God will always love us, but there has to be a time in our life when we stop and say to ourselves, "Wait, do I really want this? Or do I really want to do this? What is my walk with Jesus going to be like after this? Is this going to make me stronger? Or is this going to make me fall?"

Verses 1-7 Now the serpent was more crafty than any of the wild animals the Lord God had made. He said to the women did God really say you must not eat from any tree in the garden? The women said to the serpent we may eat fruit from the trees in the garden, but God did, say you must not eat fruit from the tree that is in the middle of the garden, and you must not touch it, or you will die. You will not certainly die the serpent said to the women. For God knows that when you eat from it your eyes will be opened, and you will be like God, knowing good and evil. When the women saw that the fruit or the tree was good for food and pleasing to the eye, and also desirable for gaining wisdom, she took some and ate it. She also gave some to her husband who was with her, and he ate it. Then the eyes of both of them were opened, and they realized they were naked; so they sewed fig leaves together and made coverings for themselves. (Genesis 3:1-7 NIV)

Verse 42 They will throw them into the blazing furnace, where there will be weeping and gnashing of teeth. (Matthew 13:42 NIV)

Hand over the Steering Wheel to Jesus

He doesn't need our help. We need his help. We think all the time that I can do this on my own, but, no, because we need him. He doesn't need us, but he wants us because he loves us, and we're his children. Rather for that he don't need us we don't do nothing for him, we can't even help him. There is only one way of helping him, and that is spreading his Word. But if you think all we do is say, "Hey, do you know Jesus?" and talk a little bit about God, then he does the rest, and the Holy Spirit takes over, so truly we can't help him. He does it all, and he doesn't need our help in life because he got it all figured out if you just let him and be patient. You must let him drive your life. Give him the steering wheel of your life. You can't just give him half. You must give him whole to truly 110 percent control of your whole life.

You can't say, "God, I trust you with my life and my future" and you're sitting down, waiting on God, but you're ready to go with anyone at any time because you figure you can hasten the process. But, no, if you give God, give it all, even down to your future. There is nothing you can do to hasten the progress. By you trying to move too fast, it can actually wreck your life in any situation. Not even marriage it could even be a job anything in life this applies to God don't need your help to figure out your life. He already got it figured out, so stop trying to play God and let God be God and do his job in your life so you can have the best life. Just be still and patient on whatever you need in life. He will give you all in time. If that's a job, kids, marriage, a home, car, whatever it is, just be patient like how he is patient with you.

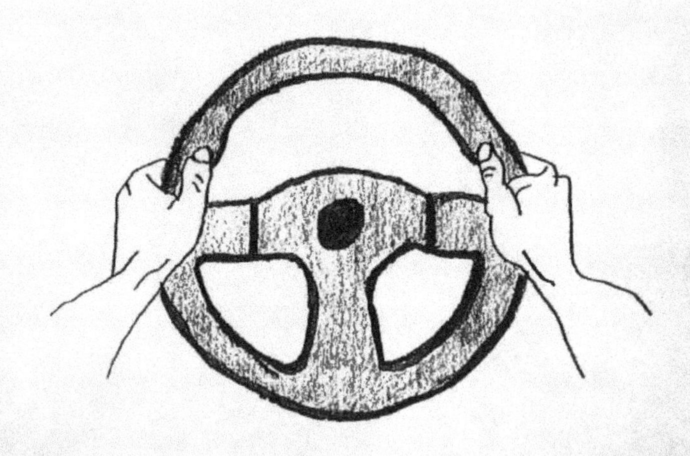

Verse 11 For I know the plans I have for you, declares the Lord, plans to prosper you and not to harm you, plans to give you hope and a future. (Jeremiah 29:11 NIV)

Verse 2 Can a man be of benefit to God? Can even a wise person benefit him? (Job 22:2 NIV)

Verse 16 You did not choose me, but I chose you and appointed you so that you might go and bear fruit-fruit that will last and so that whatever you ask in my name the Father will give you. (John 15:16 NIV)

Verses 22-23 But the fruit of the spirit is love, joy, peace, forbearance, Kindness, goodness, faithfulness, gentleness, and self-control. against such things there is no law. (Galatians 5:22-23 NIV)

Over the Rainbow

I'm driving, listening to the song, "In the River," and while I'm driving, something comes to me while I'm singing it—that storms are only temporary. While I was driving, I saw a picture of me in the pouring rain, and I'm standing outside in the rain, then all of a sudden, a rainbow came out of nowhere. It was sunny. What I got out of that was God promised us he would never flood the earth again. That's why you see a rainbow after every rainstorm. So, basically, what I got out of it was every storm has to end, and if you sit in the rain and not run from it, you will see a rainbow at the end of it. So what I'm getting at is when the STORMS come into your LIFE, you must fight against them and not go hide inside your house and wait for it to pass. You must stay and fight because at the end of the battle is a rainbow, and then you can rejoice and celebrate because the storm is over.

Verse 13 Be on your guard; stand firm in the faith; be courageous be strong. (1 Corinthians 16:13 NIV)

Verse 14 The Lord will fight for you; you need only to be still. (Exodus 14:14 NIV)

Verse 9 Have I not commanded you? Be strong and courageous. Do not be afraid; do not be discouraged, for the Lord your God will be with you wherever you go. (Joshua 1:9 NIV)

SOS

I'm just a nobody trying to tell everybody about a SOMEBODY who saved my soul. That's a big phrase, "SAVED MY SOUL." That's deep. If you stop and think what it means, saved my soul, it means someone actually saved your life, but not just anyone, it was our Lord and Savior, his Son, Jesus Christ. He died for us. He saved our souls. He basically saved our lives because without him dying for us, we would be down the road to destruction. Yes, God our Father is the same God in the Bible as he is now and before. Jesus died for us but, back then, we had to sacrifice something to God so he could forgive us for whatever sin we committed. But since he sent Jesus, he was the ultimate sacrifice, so all we have to do is ask God to forgive us, instead of sacrificing something because he already sent his Son to die for us.

So that song is accurately deep and so true. We're just nobody, and we should go and tell everybody about a somebody who saved our souls or in my words, "Who SAVED OUR LIFE." The spiritual realm is real. And by Jesus doing what he did, and by God sending his Son to do what he did literally saved our lives, and we still fail him every day and every second. But that doesn't matter to Jesus because he would still go and do it again, just so he can save our souls. And so that's why we should go and tell everybody about somebody named Jesus Christ who saved our souls because he went and died for us so we can be forgiven by the Father in the heaven and spend eternal life in heaven with him and so everybody can know about him and his Father. So what we can do at least is do what God wants us to do, and that is go and spread his Word.

Verse 21 She will give birth to a son, and you are to give him the name Jesus, because he will save his people from their sins. (Matthew 1:21 NIV)

Verse 16 For God so loved the world that he gave his one and only son, that whoever believes in him shall not perish but have eternal life. (John 3:16 NIV)

Verse 14 And we have seen and testify that the Father has sent his son to be the savior of the world. (1 John 4:14 NIV)

Pinky Promise

Peace is a promise he keeps. God will never break a promise. We break deals with him all the time, and he constantly forgives us every time, but God will never break a promise. When he says it, he means it. No matter what it is or the circumstance, God will always keep his word. Whatever he told you, he is going to do it. We don't know when or how, but he always comes through with his word. It even says in the Bible. Not only does it say it in the Bible, but he also shows himself to us that he keeps his word to us by doing whatever he told you he was going to do. But again, it's all in his timing. We all may not like how long we've got to wait or how long you have been stuck in this situation, but in time, God is going to keep his promise that he gave you. He never breaks a promise. He is not that type of God. There is no other God but him. He isn't that type to break deals or doesn't mean his word. It even says in the Bible, "Let your yes be yes, and your no be no." So just sit tight and keep the faith. God doesn't back out of deals or doesn’t finish what he started. He always ends everything he starts because he never breaks deals.

Verse 11 The Lord gives strength to his people; the Lord blesses his people with peace. (Psalm 29:11 NIV)

Verse 35 You were shown these things so that you might known that the Lord is God; besides him there is no other.

Verse 39 Acknowledge and take to heart this day that the Lord is God in heaven above and on the earth below. There is no other. (Deuteronomy 4:35, 39 NIV)

Verses 44-45 The Lord gave them rest on every side, just as he had sworn to their ancestors. Not one of their enemies withstood them; the Lord gave all their enemies into their hands. Not one of all the Lord's good promises to Israel failed; everyone was fulfilled. (Joshua 21:44-45 NIV)

Ready or Not

For we don’t know the time or the hour. That’s what the Bible says. Even his own Son, Jesus, doesn’t know when he will come back and take us home. Yeah, I know we heard it a hundred times, “Get ready. He is coming back soon.” He can come tonight, tomorrow, or in the morning. We don’t know. People say it so much, but we always overlook it. But, no, if you sit and think for a minute, God doesn’t lie or his Son, Jesus, and they left us the Bible so we can have a guide in life so we can live with him in heaven forever and get to know who created us.

So my point is, if the Bible says God’s Son—his Son who he loves and is just as equal as him and, he doesn’t even know the hour or day—then who are we to think we can sit and think we can make it another day on this earth without talking to God or reading or even talking about him? To someone it says, not theses exact words, but Jesus went back and is preparing a place for us, which means a room for us in heaven. So if Jesus, the Son of God, is even waiting every day, every hour patiently, and has no clue when his people are coming home to heaven, then who are we where we can't be prepared and wait for our Lord God to come and get us? I mean, we wait on everything we desire in our hearts, and we get prepared for it before it even comes. Like as an example now, God and Jesus loves children, but all I'm saying is if we get excited and get everything prepared for its arrival, and we get the clothes, we pick the name, we fix the room up, and it's not even here yet, why do we do that? Because we love it and we are so excited to see it.

Well, that's just like Jesus. He's so excited and happy to see us. He went and prepared a place for everyone on this earth. So all I'm saying is if Jesus doesn't know, and we're no better than him, and he is getting himself prepared, then we should too. We should start being grateful for every day because every day, God wakes you up not for your own benefit but for his benefit so we can go and spread his Word across the nations so no one gets left behind.

Verse 32 But about that day or hour no one knows, not even the angels in heaven, nor the son, but only the Father. (Mark 13:32 NIV)

Verse 42 Therefore keep watch, because you do not know on what day your Lord will come.
Verse 44 So you also must be ready, because the Son of Man will come at an hour when you do not expect him. (Matthew 24:42, 44 NIV)

Verses 2-3 My Father's house has many rooms; if that were not so, would I have told you that I am going there to prepare a place for you? And if I go and prepare a place for you, I will come back and take you to be with me that you also may be where I am. (John 14:2-3 NIV)

Meaning of True Love

I'm lying in my cousin's room, praying to myself because I have a headache, and I was saying, I'm sorry, God, for not writing last night. Then, out of nowhere, the word *love* came in my mind. So I felt I had to write about it. So what is love? Love is something you can't explain. Love is unexplainable. It's feelings toward something or someone, and you can't express yourself toward it unless by saying, "I love you." But if you sit and think what is love and what it really means, it's basically saying I care for you. But *love* is stronger word for, again, I care for you. When you love something, you show kindness toward that person or thing. You show compassion toward it and a lot of other stuff toward whatever you love. Why? Because you love it. So everything I just said is so true because no one knows what love is. But our Father in heaven does because he sent his Son, Jesus Christ, to die on the cross for us.

Now how do we know what love is? Because God showed us what love is by giving his one and only Son to die for us so we can live in heaven with him and to have everlasting life. Now if you sit and think what is God's Son about? Well, Jesus is kind, caring, he has compassion toward people, peace, love, joy, and so much more. I can't think, but everything I just said about Jesus, he is love. Without Jesus, we wouldn't know how to love or what love is. God sent him to DIE FOR US so there is one example of love. And God gives us so many other examples in life, but Jesus is love, and without Jesus, we wouldn't know how to love or even what it is because LOVE is everything I just said about.

Jesus's love is when you care for something, when something gives you joy and makes you happy. It's just unexplainable. Love is so unexplainable. It's just like how God is unexplainable. He is so amazing. There are no words, nothing to express the way he is unexplainable. In the Bible, it shows us how to love from Jesus because Jesus tells us how to be in life and how to love one another. Love is very strong. When your heart loves something so much, you will do anything for whatever it is you love. Just like God gave his only Son, his one and only Child, to die for us people on this sinful earth because he loves us so much with all his heart, and it's an unexplainable love where no one could understand how much he loves us.

If there is only one person on this earth, he would have still sent Jesus because he loves everyone, and Jesus, too, even if it was one, he still would have done it because that's true, he sacrificed his own self because he has so much love for us. I believe love is deep because Jesus and God are deep. Like I said, we only know how to love from them, no one else. God showed us the ultimate love story I would call it. His Son walked this earth and told everyone how to be and also showed it very well how to love. What is love? I may say again, love is an unexplainable feeling toward something you love. I still can't explain it because there is nothing for it. But the words *unexplainable* and *love* don't always mean relationships. You can love anything: an animal, your children, house, car, and so much more. But when you love something, you take care of it and you want to protect it well. Just like Jesus, he wants to take care of us and protect us so that's why I can answer my own question, "What is love?"

Love is Jesus Christ, our Lord and Savior. Also, love is sweet, just like Jesus. The definition of Jesus is love, so to love something, you must love Jesus first so that you know what true love is. If you don't know Jesus, then how do you know about love when Jesus is love? So to find the meaning of love, you must know the meaning of Jesus first, then from him, you will know what love is.

Verse 16 This is how we know what love is: Jesus Christ laid down his life for us. And we ought to lay down our lives for our brothers and sisters. (1 John 3:16 NIV)

Verse 16 And so, we know and rely on the love God has for us. God is love. Whoever lives in love lives in God, and God in them. (1 John 4:16 NIV)

Verse 19 We love because he first loved us. (1 John 4:19 NIV)

Do You Believe?

"And without faith it is impossible to please God, because anyone who comes to him must believe that he exists and that he rewards those who earnestly seek him" (Hebrews 11:6 NIV).

I take that as when you talk to God, you must believe in him first because if you know the Messiah is real and so is his Father, why wouldn't you believe if you know he is real? Another thing it says to me, when you seek the Lord with all your heart and mind and soul, he will reward you for seeking him because he gave us free will. That's huge. We don't have to see or love him because he gave us free will. There's a difference between "I have to" and "I'm supposed to." Have to means you're forced to whatever it is, and supposed to means you should to do it. There's a difference, and God doesn't force himself on anyone. He is a gentleman, and, yes, we are supposed to love and worship him, but because of free will, he gives us a choice. He made our life and planned our future, but we choose our choices—God's way or earthly way or even my way. So what I'm saying is God rewards us for seeking him because we choose to love him and follow him, and that's why we get rewarded.

Verse 29 Then Jesus told him, "Because you have seen me, you have believed; blessed are those who have not seen and yet have believed." (John 20:29 NIV)

Verses 9-11 If you declare with your mouth, "Jesus is Lord," and believe in your heart that God raised him from the dead, you will be saved. For it is with your heart that you believe and are justified, and it is with your mouth that you profess your faith and are saved. As scripture says, "Anyone who believes in him will never be put to shame." (Romans 10:9-11 NIV)

Verse 4 Take delight in the Lord, and he will give you the desires of your heart. (Psalm 37:4 NIV)

Construction Site

Rebuilder. What is that? It's a person who rebuilds things. As an example, a construction worker builds houses, but a rebuilder is a person who rebuilds. God is our construction worker and then works on our heart, mind, and soul, every part of the body. Not just our body, he works on our life. He rebuilds us in every way. When we feel hopelessness, brokenness, bitterness, upset, brokenhearted, anything that's not of God or even you're not good enough for him—that's the biggest lie from the devil. He makes you feel not good enough so you don't talk to God. But, anyway, when we feel broken, we're just like a broken falling house, and the only way to fix a broken house is by a construction man. Well, Jesus is our construction man. He comes and rebuilds us into something new.

Verses 17-18 But I will restore you to health and heal your wounds; declares the Lord, because you are called an out-cast, Zion for whom no one cares. This is what the Lord says.' I will restore the fortunes of Jacobs tents and have compassion on his dwellings; the city will rebuild on her ruins, and the palace will stand in its proper place. (Jeremiah 30:17-18 NIV)

Verses 2-3 The Lord builds up Jerusalem, he gathers the exiles of Israel. He heals the brokenhearted and binds up their wounds. (Psalm 147:2-3 NIV)

Verse 17 Therefore, if anyone is in Christ, the new creation has come: the old has gone, the new is here! (2 Corinthians 5:17 NIV)

Strong Foundation

Build your house on the rock, not on the sand. I always thought when I was small that meant when you get older and get married in life, you must build your family on Jesus and have your home on him and have trust in him. Well, I just thought of this. Not that it means only when you're married. Jesus is saying, in my eyes, basically, you must put your whole life on the rock, not the sand because if you put your trust in him, you won't fall. But if you're lukewarm, going back and forth, your life is going to fall, just like it said in the Bible. In my own words, when you build your house on the sand to stand, it won't stand. It will fall. On the rock, you will not fall. We must get in touch with Jesus and trust and have faith in him so our house doesn't fall.

Verses 24-27 Therefore, everyone who hears these words of mine and puts them into practice is like a wise man who builds his house on the rock. The rain came down, the streams rose, and the winds blew and beat against that house; yet it did not fall, because it had its foundation on the rock. But everyone who hears these words of mine and does not put them into practice is like a foolish man who built his house on sand. The rain came down, the streams rose, and the winds blew and beat against that house, and it fell with great crash. (Matthew 7:24-27 NIV)

Verse 48 They are like a man building a house, who dug down deep and laid the foundation on rock. When a flood came, the torrent struck that house but could not shake it, because it was well built. (Luke 6:48 NIV)

Verse 20 Built on the foundation of the apostles and prophets, with Christ Jesus himself as the chief cornerstone. (Ephesians 2:20 NIV)

Keep Going, Don't Give Up

You got to get you're again like that song a lot of people, including myself, think once you open your Bible or say one prayer a day, oh you're good, you're going to see everything you pray for overnight. No, it's just like working out. If you go to the gym one or two times, you're not going to get the result you want. You've got to keep going. Just like when you're talking to God, you have got to keep going and stay focused on his Word so you can get to your goal in life to be with Jesus in heaven. And not only that, but to find your purpose in life, you have got to keep going.

It's just like working out. You think of it like you're working your spiritual spirit. If you work hard on your muscles, why not work hard on your relationship with the Lord? It's just like working out. The more you do it, the more you will see, and you won't even realize until you stop and look at yourself one day and say, "Woah! Look what happened to me!" Same thing, but only God will reveal you your gifts.

Verse 24 Do you not know that in a race all the runners run, but only one gets the prize? Run in such a way as to get the prize. (1 Corinthians 9:24 NIV)

Verse 7 But as for you, be strong and do not give up, for your work will be rewarded. (2 Chronicles 15:7 NIV)

Verse 6 We have different gifts, according to the grace given to each of us. if your gift is prophesying, then prophesy in accordance with your faith. (Romans 12:6 NIV)

Hungry Spirit

Coronavirus—let's all go run wild and crazy and go and stock up and get food. I'm on my way right now with my aunt to get food and stock up. But does this really matter? Yeah, we need food to survive, but will it really help us survive? The only food we need to survive is God's Word, the book he left us, the Bible. Yes, we need food to survive to feed our flesh, but we never think we need to feed our spirit. Not only does our flesh need to be fed, our spirit does too. If your spirit isn't fed, then your mind really isn't fed. We all think food gives our body the strength we need and current food good for certain places on your body like carrots good for the eyes. But what is really good for the eyes is the Word so we can see how God sees. I'm speaking for myself too. If we feed our spirit, we would have God in our minds and in our hearts. He will take care of this situation in His way. So feed your spirit so we can have peace in storms.

Verses 50-51 But here is the bread that comes down from heaven, which anyone may eat and not die. I am the living bread that came down from the heaven. whoever eats this bread will live forever. this bread is my flesh, which I will give for the life of the world. (John 6:50-51 NIV)

Verse 14 Rather, clothe yourself with the Lord Jesus Christ, and do not think about how to gratify the desire of the flesh. (Romans 13:14 NIV)

Verse 27 Do not work for food that spoils, but for the food that endures to eternal life, which the son of man will give you. For on him God the Father has placed his seal of approval. (John 6:27 NIV)

Run Away

We run away from God. We walk away. He doesn’t. He stays right next to us forever, but we’re the ones who walk away from him, and we think to ourselves, *Oh, God left me*. No, he didn’t. We left him. God doesn’t lie nor does his Son, Jesus. They don’t lie. They tell the truth and hold their promises. So whatever made you feel distant from God, remember you did it yourself, not him. You can only blame yourself, not God. He didn’t leave you. You left him because something didn’t go right in your life or the way you planned. Yes, it’s not right, but I, too, walk away from God and don’t even realize it.

Verse 8 The Lord himself goes before you and will be with you; he will never leave you nor forsake you. Do not be afraid; do not be discouraged. (Deuteronomy 31:8 NIV)

Verse 14 For the Lord will not reject his people; he will never forsake his inheritance. (Psalm 94:14 NIV)

Verse 12 There is a way that appears to be right, but in the end it leads to death. (Proverbs 14:12 NIV)

Temptations

So in Luke 4:2, it says that "Satan tempted Jesus for forty days," so as soon as I read that title saying Satan tempts Jesus, I automatically thought who were we if Jesus, the Son of God, got tempted from the devil himself? We are no one compared to Jesus. We are normal people. He is our Savior, and we think to ourselves, *Oh well, how can God let this happen to me? Or how can God allow the devil to do things to me*?

No, you have your own will. God doesn't want bad things to happen to you. Yes, he allows the devil to do things, but that's up to you how you go with it. See, God lets the devil tempt his Son. He knew his boy wouldn't give in. Even though he is the Son of God, he was man. He felt everything we do. He didn't eat for forty days. He probably was starving. The devil even tempted him to make the stone into bread, and he knew he was hungry. See, God knew how strong Jesus was, how strong his flesh was, and his spirit. Even though he is the King, and he knew who God was, and he knew what his job was on this earth, Jesus still prayed to God and still kept his relationship with God. He didn't get to earth and was like, "Okay, God, I got this down here. You just do your thing in heaven."

No, Jesus still kept his relationship with the Lord. I'm not saying Jesus would have given in to temptation. No, not at all. But I'm just saying one word, if Jesus, the Son of God, the King of kings got tempted by the devil, who are we? We are no better than Jesus. I believe God allows us to get tempted to see how we deal with it because he gives us free will. He knows every move we make. It's just we have got to know in our own brains like, hey, this is temptation. This isn't from God. And not give in. And this is where it comes in again. We all should try and be like Jesus because he was on the earth. His flesh and his spirit were strong.

Verses 3-4 The devil said to him, if you are the son of God tell this stone to become bread. Jesus answered, "It is written men shall not live on bread alone." (Luke 4:3-4 NIV)

Verses 1-2 Then Jesus was led by the spirit into the wilderness to be tempted by the devil. After fasting forty days and forty nights, he was hungry. (Matthew 4:1-2 NIV)

Verses 13-14 When tempted, no one should say, God is tempting me. for God cannot be tempted by evil nor does he tempt anyone, but each person is tempted when they are dragged away by their own evil desires and enticed. (James 1:13-14 NIV)

Cry for Help When in Need

Why do we only come to God when we need his help? But any other time, we don't need God. Only when we're in trouble, we need God. Kind of funny to me because I'm guilty of it. It's kind of sad we think we can get through life without God, and we don't even realize that we act like we don't need him. But in reality, when we get scared, we ask for his help. We act like he is our backup plan who we know is always going to be there, but we only use that backup plan when we're in deep, deep trouble or just scared of anything, and we want his help. That's what's horrible about us. We use God like he's our back burner. When in reality, he's supposed to be our front burner.

God lets us go so far, and he tries to stop us, but we don't listen. If you're like me, you won't stop until you get burnt. You call for God's help when he already tried to help you, but you didn't want it. No, we need to stop ignoring God's help and only want it when we need it. No, that's not how it works. We listen to him. He doesn’t listen to us. What I mean is, we don’t rule him. He rules us. We need to start listening to him on his time, not our time, and this goes for myself too.

Verse 5 I am the vine; you are the branches. if you remain in me and I in you, you will bear much fruit; apart from me you can do nothing. (John 15:5 NIV)

Verse 10 So do not fear for I am with you; do not be dismayed, for I am your God. I will strengthen you and help you I will uphold you with my righteous right hand. (Isaiah 41:10 NIV)

Verse 63 The spirit gives life the flesh counts for nothing. The words I have spoken to you they are full of the spirit and life. (John 6:63 NIV)

Trusting the True Deliveryman

Okay, so I thought about this. How come we trust in the delivery drivers? When we order online for Christmas, like how do we all put our faith and trust in this driver and be so calm, patient, and relaxed, with no worries at all? We're actually very peaceful because all we have got to do is wait to get our stuff from the door, but how come we can't put all our faith in God who made us and knows every step we make? Yet we can't trust him. We actually get very nervous and impatient, but we trust this driver who isn't God. I'm thinking right now, *Yeah, why can't I put my faith in the Lord but it's so easy to trust the deliveryman from Amazon*?

If you're thinking to yourself like I am now, wow, what am I doing? How do I trust God like I trust the deliveryman? You just have got to let him have you and believe that God has got you covered and not worry about it. Give him your worries, just like how you think the delivery guy's got you covered, and he takes off all the worriment from trying to go find something. Instead of going into the mall, all you do is go online and say, "Okay, everyone's done. No worries here. Now it's time to just chill."

Uh no, he isn't God. I think we should put our trust in God just as much we put in man, and when that man doesn't come on time, we get disappointed when our package isn't on time. But with God, he never disappoints us. He might do things in different ways than we planned, but he never disappoints. So, basically, all I'm saying is, and this goes for me too, we need to stop putting our trust in man and start trusting in the one who created us. And when we do, we will have true peace. Not just feeling calm and peaceful for a minute, but this will be a forever peace if we keep our relationship going with him. Do I know why we put our trust in man instead of God? I don't know why, I can't tell you why, but I can tell you I know all of us are guilty of trusting man instead of God.

Verse 5 Trust in the Lord with all your heart and lean not on your own understanding. (Proverbs 3:5 NIV)

Verse 7 They will have no fear of bad news; their hearts are steadfast, trusting in the Lord. (Psalm 112:7 NIV)

Verse 5 Commit your way to the Lord; trust in him and he will do this. (Psalm 37:5 NIV)

Follow the Cross

"Lead Me to the Cross" is the song I'm listening to. I never thought about it or what it's saying. So, basically, what it is saying is "lead me to the cross where your blood poured out." Right. So I thought to myself, it meant lead me to the cross so I can crucify myself, give my old self up, crucify myself so I can give you my all like the song says "bring me to my knees. I belong to you." There you need to be vulnerable to give yourself to someone. There's nothing more vulnerable than crucifying yourself. You are literally saying, "Here, Lord, take me." So that way, I think it says lead me so I can follow him to the cross and crucify myself, just like he did 'cause we're supposed to be like him.

Verse 23 For the wages of sin is death, but the gift of God is eternal life in Christ Jesus our Lord. (Romans 6:23 NIV)

Verse 24 Then Jesus said to his disciples, whoever wants to be my disciples must deny themselves and take up their cross and follow me. (Matthew 16:24 NIV)

Verse 24 Those who belong to Christ Jesus have crucified the flesh with its passions and desires. (Galatians 5:24 NIV)

Speak into Existence

I was reading in the Bible somewhere, and it says how Jesus spoke with authority and commanded the demon to come out of someone. Well, what I got out of that, when we speak, we must have authority with no hesitations and command the things we want in our life, not even bad things. We must speak LIFE OVER OUR LIFE. The tongue is very powerful. If we're supposed to be like Jesus, then we must start speaking with authority and commands in our life in anything. I'm not saying we are God. No, we can never be God, but we can be like God. I'm thinking right now as I'm writing, *Is this wrong? What I'm saying?* but I don't think so. I'm basically saying God/Jesus, they don't speak bad out of their mouths. Just like cursing, they don't curse. So if we try and be like them, how can we be when we use our tongue for wickedness and not for good?

MIRACLES BEING BLESSED
FORGIVNESS
CIAMING GOOD HEALTH
FULFILL PURPOSES OF GOD
YOUR A CHILD OF GOD
START SEEING HOW GOD SEE YOU!
CLAME YOUR SET FREE OF DRUGS
CLAMING HAPPINESS AND PEACE IN YOUR LIFE!
CLAME YOUR NOT A ALCOHOLIC
YOU WILL SEE YOUR MOUNTAIN MOVE

Verse 29 For Jesus had commanded the impure spirit to come out of the man. Many times, it had seized him, and through he was chained hand and foot and kept under guard, he had broken his chains and had been driven by the demon into solitary places. (Luke 8:29 NIV)

Verses 43-44 When he said this Jesus called in a loud voice, Lazarus come out! the dead man came out, his hands and feet wrapped with strips of linen and a cloth around his face. Jesus said to them take off the grave clothes and let him go. (John 11:43-44 NIV)

Verse 3 And God, said let there be light, and there was light. (Genesis 1:3 NIV)

Battlefield

The battle when you're a Christian seeking, it's a battle every day. Every second, it's a spiritual battle. When you're a Christian, and you're not seeking, there is no battle because what are you fighting when you're on the team you're supposed to be against? The enemy isn't fighting you when you're on his team because what are you fighting when you're on the same team? But as soon as you leave his team, oh, that's when the battle begins because he wants you on his team. Even when you aren't seeking, you're still in battle, but you don't know it because God wants you. But you can't tell because you're not looking for God. You're distracted by the enemy. Even for the nonbelievers, whatever they label themselves, they're in a battle too but don't know it either. If it's God fighting for them to come to him or the enemy messing with them, no matter what you believe, there's only one God, and the enemy is real. He does try and keep you so God won't have you!

Verse 11 Put on the full armor of God, so that you can take your stand against the devil's schemes.

Verses 14-17 Stand firm then, with the belt of truth buckled around your waist, with the breastplate of Righteousness in place, and with your feet fitted with the readiness that comes from the gospel of peace. in addition to all this, take up the shield of faith, with which you can extinguish all the flaming arrows of the evil one. take the helmet of salvation and the sword of spirit, which is the word of God. (Ephesians 6:11, 14-17 NIV)

Verse 10 The thief comes only to steal and kill and destroy; I have come that they may have life, and have it to the full. (John 10:10 NIV)

Verse 20 Here I am! I stand at the door and knock. if anyone hears my voice and opens the door, I will come in and eat with that person, and they with me. (Revelation 3:20 NIV)

Ticket into Heaven

Are we just using God to get into heaven? Or do we really want to be with him in heaven? Now that's something to really meditate on. We label ourselves as Christians, but are we loving God? Serving him in our own way? As we call serving God just to get into heaven? Or are we getting in because he's our friend and we love him? Now what I mean by serving God in our own way is that we call ourselves Christians, and we don't do the will of God. We don't act on it. We don't spread the Gospel. We just go to church or we don't go to church, and when people ask, "What do you believe?" you say, "I'm Christian, and I love Jesus." I'm not condemning anybody. There are some people who really do the works of the Lord, and there some who don't most of the time. No judgment, it's just something to really meditate about because I, too, was both Christians at one point of my life. I know the world is a very distracting place. Sometimes, we have to stop and evaluate ourselves.

When I mean evaluate, I mean search your own heart. Are these things in the word what I'm doing for the Lord? Or how about am I giving just five minutes of my day to God? When you get to that point in your life and you examine yourself, then I want you to ask yourself, which Christian am I? The one who wants Jesus in my life with no work? Or am I the Christian that wants Jesus in my life and wants to do his works? After you ask yourself that question when evaluating yourself, I want you to ask yourself, "Am I a Christian because I'm excited to spend eternity with God? Or am I a Christian just because Jesus died on the cross for me, and I got an easy ticket into heaven with no strings attached?" I asked myself before all the same questions I'm asking you to ask yourself. From me analyzing myself, that's how I'm writing this book right now about our Lord and Savior.

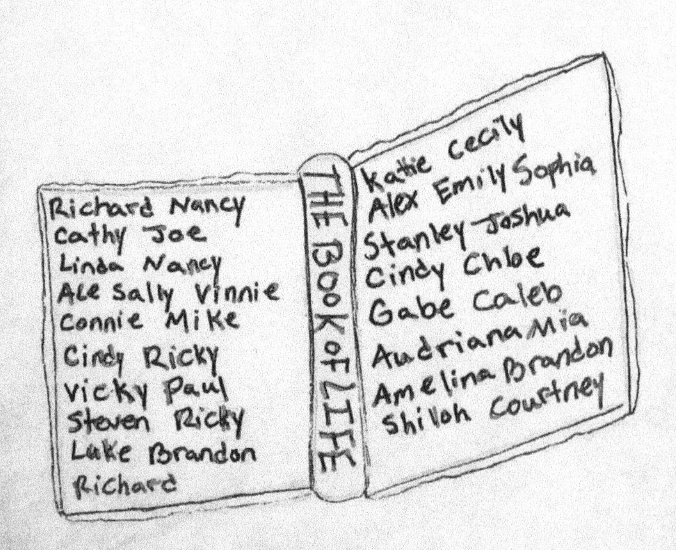

Verse 21 Not everyone who says to me, "Lord, Lord" will enter the Kingdom of heaven but only the one who does the will of my father who is in heaven. (Matthew 7:21 NIV)

Verse 45 For even the son of man did not come to be served, but to serve, and to give his life as a ransom for many. (Mark 10:45 NIV)

Verse 13 For he has rescued us from the dominion of darkness and brought us into the Kingdom of the son he loves. (Colossians 1:13 NIV)

God's Will Will Be Done

It's crazy how God's will works out at the end of the night. I'm just chilling, lying in my bed, thinking how a week before Jesus was crucified, the same exact people who were screaming hosanna, laying down palms for him, loved him and were so happy. But it's funny how a week later, seven days later, they hated him and wanted to murder him. I'm just thinking, maybe if they would have kept loving him and not hating him, who would have killed Jesus then? And there would have been no ultimate sacrifice. So I believe God planned all along to have the same exact people to crucify him because you can't kill anything you love, and if they all truly loved Jesus, then Barabbas would have died, not Jesus.

Verse 17 So, when the crowd had gathered Pilate asked them, which one do you want me to release to you; Jesus Barabbas, or Jesus who is called the Messiah? (Matthew 27:17 NIV)

Verses 13-14 They took palm branches and went out to meet him, shouting "hosanna!" "Bless is he who comes in the name of the Lord!" "Blessed is the king of Israel!" Jesus found a young donkey and sat on it, as it is written. (John 12:13-14 NIV)

Verse 42 Father, if you are willing take this cup from me; yet not my will, but yours be done. (Luke 22:42 NIV)

Wait on the Lord

God waits for us all the time, 24-7, but do we wait for him? That's the question here. Do we wait for him? I don't think so because if we waited for him, we would be ready for him 24-7, like how he is ready for us 24-7. God patiently waits for us. He sits and waits for us to come to him. He doesn't force himself on to us. He's a gentleman. So I ask again, do we wait on God? No, we don't. If we would wait on God, we wouldn't mind waiting for our prayers to be answered instead of getting aggravated when we don't get our prayers answered fast enough. So if we wait on God like how he waits on us, we would have the patience like God does and wouldn't doubt God like how he don't doubt us.

He puts his faith that we won't fail him in anything we do. But we do fail him all the time because we are sinners. But God loves us anyway, and he still waits patiently for us to come and hang with him and to show him love. He just wants 5 percent, not even 10. God wants to feel loved just like anyone else. He loves us so much. It's unexplainable. So all he asks is just for you to talk to him for one minute instead of talking to him when you need worldly things. Yes, He loves when you ask for stuff, but sometimes, God wants to just talk to you like how you talk to your friends because he wants to be your friend.

Verse 15 I no longer call you servants, because a servant does not know his master's business. instead, I have called you friends, for everything that I learned from my father I have made known to you. (John 15:15 NIV)

Verse 18 Yet the Lord longs to be gracious to you; therefore, he will rise up to show you compassion. for the Lord is a God of justice. Bless are all who wait for him! (Isaiah 30:18 NIV)

Verse 9 The Lord is not slow in keeping his promise, as some understand slowness. Instead, he is patient with you not wanting anyone to perish, but everyone to come to repentance. (2 Peter 3:9 NIV)

Rainbow of Promise

Everyone knows when it rains, a rainbow comes after. Well, God made that promise to Noah years ago, centuries ago, and still, today, every time it rains, a rainbow shows up. So, basically, if God makes a promise to you, or in general, he promises something to you, just wait, it will happen. He never backs out on a promise. He always comes through. If he made a promise years and years ago, saying he would never flood earth again, and, still, to this day kept his word, he will do the same with any promises. God is the same today as he was years ago.

Verses 11-16 I establish My covenant with you; never again will all life be destroyed by the waters of a flood; never again will there be a flood to destroy the earth. And God said, "this is the sign of the covenant I am making between me and you and every living creature with you, a covenant for all generations to come; I have set my rainbow in the clouds, and it will be the sign of the covenant between me and the earth. Whenever I bring clouds over the earth and the rainbow appears in the clouds, I will remember my covenant between me and you and all living creatures of every kind never again will the waters become a flood to destroy all life. Whenever the rainbow appears in the clouds, I will see it and remember the everlasting covenant between God and all living creatures of every kind on the earth." (Genesis 9:11-16 NIV)

Verse 20 For no matter how many promises God has made they are "yes" in Christ. And so through him the "Amen" is spoken by us to the glory of God. (2 Corinthians 1:20 NIV)

Verse 13 Your Kingdom is an everlasting Kingdom, and your dominion endures through all generations. the Lord is trustworthy in all he promises and faithful in all he does. (Psalm 145:13 NIV)

Prideful

Pride. What do you think of when you hear the word *pride*? Do you think of gay people now? Or do you think of someone who is prideful of their self? I'll be honest, I hear pride so much I think of the gays. Just think how evil the devil is. He took God's promised rainbow and turned it into a gay flag. He also took the word *pride* and made it a good thing to some people, which actually isn't a good thing because God doesn't like the prideful. He likes when his children are humble and not selfish, like his Son, Jesus.

So what I'm trying to say is, the devil is a liar and a manipulator. He takes bad things and makes us believe it's good, just like the word *pride.* You hear that saying, "Swallow your pride." Well, no one thinks of that saying anymore. We all think Pride Month or rainbow stuff, and I don't mean God's promise, I mean gay stuff. Sounds horrible to say, but there's no other way to say it. So, basically, the devil will try and make all this look good when, actually, it's not, and it's everything God is not about. So don't let the enemy try and distract you, even if it’s a certain word because he also made *pride* seem to be another word for happy when it’s not. Pride leads to destruction.

Verses 9-10 Or do you not know that wrongdoers will not inherit the Kingdom of God? Do not be deceived; neither the sexually immoral nor idolaters nor adulterers nor men who have sex with men. Nor thieves nor the greedy nor drunkards nor slanderers nor swindlers will inherit the Kingdom of God. (1 Corinthians 6:9-10 NIV)

Verse 18 Pride goes before destruction, a haughty spirit before a fall. (Proverbs 16:18 NIV)

Verse 4-5 To the arrogant I say, boast no more, and to the wicked, do not lift up your horns. Do not lift your horns against heaven; do not speak so defiantly. (Psalm 75:4-5 NIV)

Perfect Timing

Waiting, waiting on the Lord. If we would only just wait on the Lord like how we would wait for someone to ring our phone, meaning a doctor, a friend, anyone, we would be just fine. We wait patiently all day, all night, for a certain call. Sometimes that call comes that day, sometimes it doesn't, or it comes the next day or two. Either way, we still wait, and we are preparing ourselves for that phone to ring. So imagine if we prepared ourselves for Jesus's coming back? Or just patiently waiting on God's timing? If we can patiently wait and wait and think about that phone ringing, why can't we do the same with God? And this goes for me too. Why can't I just patiently wait on God? And we can't keep blaming, "Oh, we're human. I'm flesh."

Jesus was too, and he got tempted. We're supposed to be like Jesus. So all I'm saying is try your hardest to deny sin because we are not perfect like God or Jesus, but we could try and be like Jesus like God wants. So, basically, we play the waiting game all the time in life with everything, and we're cool with it. Yes, we get aggravated sometimes waiting in line or waiting for a phone call, but we still wait. So if you just wait a little longer in your situation, it will come to an end all in good timing and for good. So if we wait on him on his timing, we win at the end of the night, which by winning, I mean, be with Jesus and God in heaven forever.

Verses 1-13 At that time the Kingdom of heaven will be like 10 virgins who took their lamps and went out to meet the bride-groom. five of them were foolish and five were wise. the fool-ish ones took their lamps but did not take any oil with them. the wise ones, however, took oil and jars along with their lamps. the bridegroom was a long time in coming and they all became drowsy and fell asleep, at mid-night the cry rang out here's the bridegroom! come out to meet him! Then all the virgins woke up and trimmed their lamps. the foolish one said to the wise, give us some of your oil; our lamps are going out. no, they replied There may not be enough for both of us and you. Instead, go to those who sell oil and buy some for yourself. but while they were on their way to buy the oil the bridegroom arrived. The virgins who were ready went in with him to the wedding banquet; and the door was shut. later the others also came. Lord, Lord they said open the door for us! but he replied truly I tell you I don't know you. therefore, keep watch because you don't know the day or hour. (Matthew 25:1-13 NIV)

Verse 14 Wait for the Lord; be strong and take heart and wait for the Lord. (Psalm 27:14 NIV)

Verse 6 Do not be anxious about anything, but in every situation, by prayer and petition, with thanksgiving present your requests to God. (Philippians 4:6 NIV)

Verse 1 I waited patiently for the Lord; he turned to me and heard my cry. (Psalm 40:1 NIV)

Blessing

Blessings. What is a blessing? When you hear the word *blessing,* what do you think of? I automatically think of someone giving you something when you need it or you just wanted it, and someone goes out of their way to buy it for you unexpectedly or someone just wanted to be nice and gave you something. Well, that's just like with God, except it's not just from anyone, it's from our Lord. He gives us gifts.

Now do we know why he does this? Even though we don't deserve it, he blesses us because he loves us and wants us to have everything, not even money or stuff we want. He blesses us by our health, also with everything in life. He blessed us with even sending Jesus, his Son, to die for us. That was a blessing because Jesus loves us so much. He was willing to die for us so God can have grace on us. So we should be thankful for everything and every day because we are all blessed and we serve an amazing graceful giving God who wants to bless his kids more and more, not just one time. I feel he will continue to bless you until he comes back or until you go home to the Lord.

Verses 24-26 The Lord bless you and keep you, the Lord make his face shine on you and be gracious to you the Lord turned his face toward you and give you peace. (Numbers 6:24-26 NIV)

Verse 17 Every good and perfect gift is from above, coming down from the Father of the heavenly lights, who does not change like shifting shadows. (James 1:17 NIV)

Verses 19-20 And my God will meet all your needs according to the riches of his glory in Christ Jesus. to our God and Father be glory forever and ever Amen. (Philippians 4:19-20 NIV)

God Is 24-7, Never Closes

Just like that song, "He Never Stops Working," it's true, God never stops working. We stop working, we stop putting effort in God. It's a relationship, just like it says, even when we don't see it. That's true, too, when we don't see it, when we don't know how it's going to change or work out, he's working it out behind the scenes. That's up to us to keep walking with him, putting time and effort in because while he's working stuff out in our life, that's him putting effort into us. So we want and want, but we put zero effort back when God is constantly 24-7 working for us, and we can't give him 10 percent. So next time you think it's not going to work out, or where is God? Remember, he is working. The teacher is always silent when the students are in a test. He never leaves us. We leave him.

So give God a chance. Don't walk away when life gets hard. We need him in bad and good days. Give him a chance like how he gives us chances. We don't allow God to be God. We want it when we want it and how we want it. If we allow God to be him like how he allows us to be ourselves, and if we truly trust him and have faith and believe he's going to do it because that's what his Word says, you will have it. He wants us to have everything our heart desires, but God only desires our hearts and for us to truly love him, nothing else. So when you sacrifice your life and truly search and seek him, you will find the Lord, and he will give you more than you ask for in his time.

Verse 12 It is a land the Lord your God cares for; the eyes of the Lord your God are continually on it from the beginning of the year to its end. (Deuteronomy 11:12 NIV)

Verses 20-23 My prayer is not for them alone. I pray also for those who will believe in me through their message, that all of them may be one, Father, just as you are in me, and I am and you. may they also be in us so that the world may believe that you have sent me. I have given them the glory that you gave me, that they may be one as we are one. I in them and you in me so that they may be brought to complete unity. then the world will know that you sent me and have loved them even as you have loved me. (John 17:20-23 NIV)

Verse 8 And God is able to bless you abundantly, so that in all things at all times, having all that you need, you will abound in every good work. (2 Corinthians 9:8 NIV)

Best Friend Forever

"Friends come and go," they say. But you know what doesn't come and go? That's God and his Son, Jesus. They stay. So the only friend you need is God. He stays with you until the end. He will never leave you. We leave him, but he doesn't leave us. God and his Son wants to be our friend. He is a gentleman. No forcing. He just wants to be friends with you, have relationship with him, and get to know him like how he knows us. Don't you want to know all about the God who created you? I mean, he thought about creating you. It was in his mind to make you have life, so don't you wonder what he is like? He knows us inside and out. He just wants us to know him and take him close and love him just as much as he loves us.

I mean, he thought of me and had to make me. He already knew me when he made me, but he wanted to give me life because he loves me, if that makes sense. And the same for the world, he thought of you then made you because he loved you. So, God and his Son just want to be your friend. You love your friends because you take your time to get to know your friends. So take some time and get to know your Lord and his Son, our Savior.

Verse 5 Keep your life free from the love of money and be content with what you have, because God has said "never will I leave you; never will I forsake you." (Hebrews 13:5 NIV)

Verse 23 And the scriptures was fulfilled that says, Abraham believed God, and it was credited to him as righteousness, and he was called God's friend. (James 2:23 NIV)

Verse 5 Before I formed you in the womb I knew you, before you were born I set you apart; I appointed you as a prophet to the nations. (Jeremiah 1:5 NIV)

Childlike Faith

The Bible talks about childlike faith. You must have childlike faith to enter the kingdom of heaven. When you were a child, didn't you think you can do anything? You could jump off the swing to the playground, not even thinking you're going to break a leg. But as an adult, you're more careful. You know what you're doing as an adult. By jumping off the swings, you might get seriously hurt. We get scared. But when you're a child, you have no fear, and you believe anything your parents told you. If your parents told you a dog is a cat, you're going to believe a dog is a cat. That's how God wants us to be. We have to go back to our childlike ways to believing and not having fear, and yes, trusting our parents' word, that's it. It's true. Same exact thing with God. We have to believe like a child and just believe and trust in him like how we do with our parents. He is our heavenly Father. It is the same exact thing.

Verse 3 And he said truly I tell you, unless you change and become like little children, you will never enter the Kingdom of heaven. (Matthew 18:3 NIV)

Verses 14-15 When Jesus saw this, he was indignant. he said to them, "let the little children come to me, and do not hinder them, for the Kingdom of God belongs to such as these. truly I tell you, anyone who will not receive the Kingdom of God like a little child will never enter it." (Mark 10:14-15 NIV)

Verse 20 He replied, "Because you have so little faith. truly I tell you, if you have faith as small as a mustard seed, you can say to this mountain, 'move from here to there.' And it will move. nothing will be impossible for you." (Matthew 17:20 NIV)

Endless Lives

I'm playing a game on my phone, and it says, "You got endless lives." So I thought to myself, *Imagine if in real life I got endless lives, what would I do*? That's a long time. Then I said to myself, *You do have an endless life in real life*. When you believe in Jesus Christ, he gives you life, and he gives you eternal life, which means forever alive. We all know life isn't like a game or a fairy-tale book, but once you give your life to the Lord and learn who he is, it's the greatest love story of all time, better than anything you ever read before. Only Jesus can give you eternal life. If you want endless lives, get to know him and surrender all to him.

Verses 8-9 Phillip said, "Lord, show us the father and that will be enough for us." Jesus answered: don't you know me, Phillip, even after I have been among you such a long time? anyone who has seen me has seen the Father. how can you say, 'show us the Father?' (John 14:8-9 NIV)

Verse 35 Then Jesus declared, "I am the bread of life. whoever comes to me will never go hungry, and whoever believes in me will never be thirsty." (John 6:35 NIV)

Verse 7 Then the Lord God formed a man from the dust of the ground and breathed into his nostrils the breath of life, and the man became a living being. (Genesis 2:7 NIV)

Fiery Flames

Did you ever get in the shower, and the water is way too hot? And you get into the shower and you screamed? Or you automatically flinched away from the water, and you turned the water down cooler? So if that burns, can you imagine what hell feels like? Constantly burning on your skin. You can't change it from hot to cold either. You're stuck with that forever and ever, constantly, 24-7, nonstop of fiery flames all over, can't get away from the heat. Forget about hot water. What happens to you when you're outside, and it's scorching hot outside? You get automatically thirsty. Imagine if your body felt like an oven all the time, and you couldn't get anything to drink. That would be torture.

In hell, you won't get a drink. All you get is torture and unexplainable heat. So in this horrible place, you will drive for the taste of water. A drizzle even, just to probably cool you down, but sadly, you won't ever cool down, you will only burn forever. And there's some people who think earth is hell. Earth is far from it. Hell is no place to be. So you're hot, thirsty, and tortured, 24-7. It doesn't sound like a happy place to me. It sounds like a terrifying place to me.

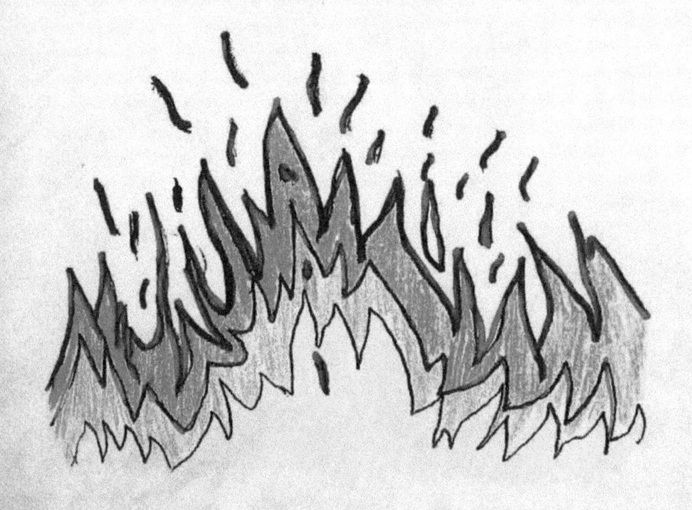

Verses 23-24 In Hades, where he was in torment, He looked up and saw Abraham far away, with Lazarus by his side. So he called to him, "Father Abraham, have pity on me and send Lazarus to dip the tip of his finger in water and cool my tongue, because I am in agony in this fire." (Luke 16:23-24 NIV)

Verses 27-28 He answered, "Then I beg you, father, send Lazarus to my family, for I have five brothers. let him warn them, so that they will not also come to this place of torment." (Luke 16:27-28 NIV)

Verse 11 As for you, because of the blood of my covenant with you, I will free your prisoners from the waterless pit. (Zechariah 9:11 NIV)

Verse 20 But the beast was captured, and with its the false prophet who had performed the signs on its behalf. with these signs he had deluded those who had received the mark of the beast and worshiped its image. The two of them were thrown alive into the fiery lake of burning sulfur. (Revelation 19:20 NIV)

I AM

	Gal 3:26-29
a child of the Most High God	Psalms 82:6
fearfully and wonderfully made	Psalms 139:14
born of God + the evil one can NOT touch me	1 John 5:18
co-heirs with Christ	Rom. 8:17
adopted as His child	Eph 1:5
a citizen of Heaven	Phil 3:20
Chosen, even before the creation of the world	Eph 1:4+11
sealed with the Holy Spirit	Eph 1:13
blessed in the heavenly realms with EVERY spiritual blessing	Eph 1:3
the head and not the tail	Deut 28:13
accepted and loved	Eph 1:6
a dwelling place for the Holy Spirit	Eph 2:22
alive in Christ	Eph 2:5
God's workmanship	Eph 2:10
not in want	Phil 4:19
holy and blameless	Eph 1:4
dead to sin	Rom 6:11
set free	Rom 8:2
redeemed	Gal 3:13
victorious	1 John 5:4
More than a conqueror	Rom 8:37
born again	1 Peter 1:23
a new creation	2 Cor. 5:17
God's prized possession	Deut 7:6
Prayed for by Jesus Christ!	John 17:20-23

Fruit of the Spirit's
- Joy
- Love
- peace
- Kindness
- goodness
- faithfulness
- gentleness
- self control
- patience

Isaiah 54:17

"No weapon formed against you shall prosper,
And every tongue which rises against you in judgement You shall condemn.
This is the heritage of the servants of the Lord, and their righteousness is from Me
Says the Lord.

About the Author

Monica Gilk was born December 19, 2000, in New Jersey. She lives with her mom, dad, and brother. *Letters from God* is the first book she ever wrote at the age of twenty-one. She enjoys going to the beach, riding roller coasters, and planting flowers and fruits in her yard. She loves the smells of flowers. Her two favorite flowers are peony and roses. Monica loves all of her friends that she is constantly with. Monica's friends did her makeup, hair, and photoshoot for the *Letters from God* book. She calls them her glam squad. Monica is very excited, hoping everyone who reads *Letters from God* receives and enjoys reading it.

Lightning Source UK Ltd.
Milton Keynes UK
UKHW021151160123
415417UK00011B/137